Anne of Green Gables

Lucy Maud Montgomery

Level 2

Retold by Anne Collins
Series Editors: Andy Hopkins and Jocelyn Potter

Pearson Education Limited
Edinburgh Gate, Harlow,
Essex CM20 2JE, England
and Associated Companies throughout the world.

Pack ISBN: 978-1-4058-5205-0
Book ISBN: 978-1-4058-4273-0
CD-ROM ISBN: 978-1-4058-5054-4

First published by Harrap 1925
First published by Penguin Books 2002
This edition published 2007

1 3 5 7 9 10 8 6 4 2

Text copyright © Penguin Books Ltd 2002
This edition copyright © Pearson Education Ltd 2007
Illustrations by Sally Cutting

Set in 12/15.5pt A. Garamond
Printed in China
SWTC/01

Produced for the Publishers by AC Estudio Editorial S.L.

Published by Pearson Education Ltd in association with Penguin Books Ltd,
both companies being subsidiaries of Pearson Plc

Acknowledgements
We are grateful to the following for permission to reproduce photographs:
Page 59: © Bill Brooks / Alamy (top), © eStock Photo / Alamy (middle), © Andre Jenny / Alamy (bottom).

Every effort has been made to trace the copyright holders and we apologise in advance for any
unintentional omissions. We would be pleased to insert the appropriate
acknowledgement in any subsequent edition of this publication.

For a complete list of the titles available in the Penguin Active Reading series please write to your local
Pearson Longman office or to: Penguin Readers Marketing Department, Pearson Education,
Edinburgh Gate, Harlow, Essex CM20 2JE, England.

Contents

1.1 What's the book about?

Talk about the picture on the front of this book.

1 How old is the girl?
2 Where is she?
3 What is she waiting for?
4 Why is nobody with her?
5 What is she thinking?
6 What is she feeling?

1.2 What happens first?

Look at the name of Chapter 1 and the sentences in *italics* on page 1. Then look at the pictures in Chapter 1 and the words at the bottom of the pages. Circle the best answers.

1 Avonlea is in … .
    the United States   (Canada)   Mexico

2 The time is … .
    the 1700s   the 1800s   the 1900s

3 The girl and the man go to the house … .
    by train   by car   by horse and buggy

4 The girl is about … .
    eleven   fourteen   nineteen

5 The man is … .
    the girl's father   the girl's uncle   a stranger

6 On the way to the house, the girl is … .
    happy   surprised   sad

7 The man is … .
    happy   surprised   sad

8 At the end of the chapter, the man and the woman are … .
    happy   excited   sad

CHAPTER 1

Anne Arrives in Avonlea

"You don't want me!" cried the child suddenly.
"You don't want me because I'm not a boy!"

One fine spring afternoon in Avonlea, Mrs. Rachel Lynde sat by her kitchen window. She often sat there because she could see the Avonlea road very well from there.

A man with a horse and **buggy** came up the road. It was Mrs. Lynde's neighbor, Matthew Cuthbert.

"Where's Matthew going?" thought Mrs. Lynde in **surprise**. "It's half past three in the afternoon and he has a lot of work on his farm. Where's he going and why is he going there?"

Matthew Cuthbert lived with his sister, Marilla, in Green Gables, a large old house near Mrs. Lynde's home. Later, Mrs. Lynde walked to Green Gables.

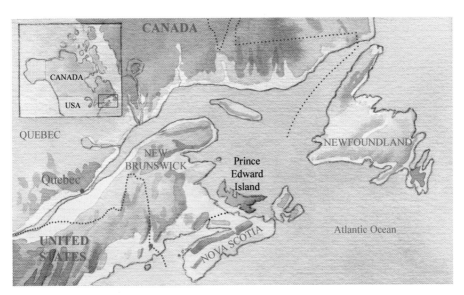

buggy /ˈbʌgi/ (n) In past times, people sat in a *buggy* and a horse pulled it.
surprise /səˈpraɪz, səˈpraɪs/ (n) When a friend plans a *surprise* for you, you don't know about it. When you learn about it, you are very *surprised*.

1

Marilla Cuthbert was busy in the kitchen. She was a tall, thin woman with gray hair. Marilla wasn't young or pretty, and she didn't smile very much. But she had a kind **heart**. She wasn't surprised by Mrs. Lynde's visit.

"Hello, Marilla," said Mrs. Lynde. "I saw Matthew on the road. Where's he going?"

"To Bright River Station," answered Marilla. "We're getting a little boy from an **orphanage** in Nova Scotia. He's coming on the train this afternoon."

Mrs. Lynde couldn't speak. Then she said, "An **orphan** boy! Why do you want an orphan boy?"

"Matthew is sixty years old," answered Marilla. "His heart isn't very strong. He wants a boy to help him on the farm.

"We heard about Mrs. Spencer at White Sands. She's getting a little girl from the orphanage. Matthew and I want a little boy. Mrs. Spencer went to the orphanage today. She's bringing a boy back on the train and she's going to leave him at the station. Matthew will meet him there."

heart /hɑrt/ (n) When your *heart* stops, you are going to die. People say that your feelings come from your *heart*.
orphan /ˈɔrfən/ (n) An *orphan* has no parents because they are dead. An *orphanage* is a home for a lot of *orphans*.

"I think you're doing a very stupid thing, Marilla," said Mrs. Lynde. "You're bringing a strange boy into your house. You don't know anything about him.

"I read a story in the newspaper about an orphan. This child lived with a Canadian family. The child lit a fire one night and the family died in the fire. But it was a girl, not a boy."

"But we're not getting a girl," said Marilla. "We don't want a girl. We're getting a boy."

Bright River Station was about twelve kilometers from Avonlea. Matthew drove there slowly in the buggy. When he arrived at Bright River, it was late. He couldn't see a train.

There was only one person at the station, a little girl about eleven years old. She was very thin with large gray eyes and long red hair. She wore a short, ugly dress and carried an old bag.

When she saw Matthew, she smiled. Then she put out her hand. "Are you Mr. Matthew Cuthbert of Green Gables?" she asked. "I'm from the orphanage. Mrs. Spencer brought me here."

Matthew took the child's hand. "There's a mistake," he thought. "This is a girl, not a boy!"

"When you weren't here at the station," said the child, "I thought, 'I can sleep in that big tree tonight. I know he'll come in the morning.' I know it's a long way to your house. Mrs. Spencer told me. But I love driving. And I'm going to have a home with you. That's wonderful. I never had a home."

"I was late," said Matthew slowly. "I'm sorry." He took the little girl's bag and they walked to the buggy. "I can't leave this child at the station," he thought. "I'll take her back to Green Gables. Marilla can tell her about the mistake."

The girl got into the buggy and Matthew drove home. The child talked and talked. Matthew listened. He was a quiet man and he was usually afraid of little girls. But he liked listening to this girl's conversation.

"Look at those trees with the beautiful white flowers," said the girl. "I love the color white. I'd like a beautiful white dress. I never had a pretty dress. They only gave us ugly clothes at the orphanage. I know I'm going to be very happy with you. But one thing makes me sad. Look at my hair. What color is it?"

"Isn't it red?" asked Matthew.

"Yes," said the little girl sadly. "It's red. I hate my red hair."

It was evening when they arrived at Green Gables. Marilla came to the door and looked at the child in surprise.

"Who's this, Matthew?" she asked. "Where's the boy?"

"There wasn't a boy," said Matthew unhappily. "There was only her. I couldn't leave her at the station."

"No boy!" said Marilla. "But we asked Mrs. Spencer for a boy!"

"You don't want me!" cried the child suddenly. "You don't want me because I'm not a boy! Oh, what shall I do?"

"Don't cry," said Marilla. "We can't send you back to the orphanage tonight. You'll have to stay here. What's your name?"

The child stopped crying. "Can you call me Cordelia?" she asked.

"Cordelia! Is that your name?" asked Marilla in surprise.

"No," said the child sadly. "But Cordelia is a prettier name than mine. My name is Anne Shirley. Anne with an 'e'. But please call me Cordelia."

"No," said Marilla, but she smiled. "Anne is a very good name. Now come and eat something, Anne."

Anne sat down at the table but she couldn't eat anything. So Marilla took her upstairs to a small bedroom. Anne took off her clothes and got sadly into bed.

Marilla went downstairs and washed the plates. Matthew sat in a chair. He didn't say very much.

"I'll drive to Mrs. Spencer's house tomorrow," said Marilla, "and I'll ask her about this mistake. We'll have to send this child back."

"She's a very nice little girl," said Matthew slowly, "and very interesting. She likes to talk. And she wants to stay with us."

Marilla was very surprised. "But, Matthew, she *can't* stay here," she said. "A girl can't help you on the farm."

"But maybe *we* can help *her*," answered Matthew quietly.

"I'm going to send her back to the orphanage," said Marilla. "I don't want an orphan girl."

"All right, Marilla," said Matthew. "I'm going to bed now."

Marilla put the plates away and went to bed, too. And in the room upstairs, the little orphan girl cried and cried.

2.1 Were you right?

Look back at Activity 1.2 on page iv. Then write notes about Matthew, Marilla, and Anne.

Name: ....

Age: ....

Problems: ..weak.......
heart..................................

Wants: ..a boy...............
to help him.......................

Name: ....

Age: ....

Hair: ....

Eyes: ....

Wants: ..a home...........

Name: ....

Hair: ....

Doesn't want: ....

....

Lives at: ..Green..........
Gables.........................

2.2 What more did you learn?

1 Are the sentences right (✓) or wrong (✗)?

a Matthew is Marilla's husband.

b Mrs. Lynde thinks an orphan boy is a good idea.

c The train arrives at the station before Matthew.

d The girl doesn't talk on the way home.

e At the orphanage the girl had only pretty dresses.

f Marilla is going to send the child back.

g The girl likes the name Anne.

h Anne is very happy at the end of her first day at Green Gables.

2 What do you think is in Anne's old bag? Talk to other students.

.3 Language in use

Look at the sentence in the box. Then put the right words in each sentence below.

"But I **love driving**!"

hate + wear	like + be	love + watch
like + work	love + talk	like + listen

1 Mrs. Lynde .... her neighbors.

2 Anne .... in the buggy.

3 Matthew .... to Anne.

4 Anne .... the ugly orphanage clothes.

5 Anne ....

6 Matthew .... on the farm.

.4 What's next?

1 At the end of Chapter 1, which of these is right? Check (✓) one sentence.

   a Matthew doesn't want Anne to stay.

   b Marilla doesn't want Anne to stay.

   c Anne doesn't want to stay.

2 Which of these will happen? Check (✓) one sentence.

   d Marilla will leave Anne with Mrs. Spencer.

   e Anne will stay at Green Gables.

   f Matthew will send Anne back to the orphanage.

3 The name of Chapter 2 is "A Sad Story." Who has a sad story, do you think? What is the story? Talk to other students.

A Sad Story

"They wanted to be kind," Anne said slowly. "But they were always very tired. They couldn't really be kind to me."

When Anne woke up the next morning, she felt happy. She jumped out of bed and ran to the window.

It was a beautiful morning. The sun shone and the sky was blue. Anne opened the window. Outside, there was a fruit tree with beautiful flowers. Anne could see many other trees and flowers, and a small river, too.

"This is a wonderful place!" she thought. Then, suddenly, she remembered. She felt very sad again. "But I can't stay here," she thought. "They don't want me because I'm not a boy."

Marilla came into the room. "Good morning, Anne," she said. "Breakfast is waiting. Wash your face and put on your clothes."

"I'm feeling very hungry," Anne said. "I can never be sad in the mornings. I love mornings."

After breakfast, Anne washed the plates and cups. Marilla watched carefully, but Anne did the job well.

"This afternoon I'm going to drive to White Sands," Marilla said. "You'll come with me, Anne, and we'll talk to Mrs. Spencer."

Matthew didn't say anything, but he looked very sad. Later, he got the horse and buggy ready for Marilla. Marilla drove, and Anne sat next to her.

"Is it a long way to White Sands?" asked Anne.

"About eight kilometers," answered Marilla. "I know you like to talk, Anne. So tell me your story."

"It isn't very interesting," said Anne. "I was born in Bolingbroke in Nova Scotia, and I was eleven last March. My parents were teachers. But they died when I was a baby. So their cleaner, Mrs. Thomas, and her husband took me into their house.

"Mrs. Thomas had four children. I helped her with them. But then Mr. Thomas died in an accident. Mrs. Thomas and the children went to Mr. Thomas's parents. They didn't want me.

"Then Mrs. Hammond, Mrs. Thomas's friend, took me into her house. She had eight children. They were very hard work. Then Mrs. Hammond moved away. I had to go to the orphanage because nobody wanted me. I was there for four months."

"Did you go to school?" asked Marilla.

"No, not often," answered Anne. "I didn't have time. I was always busy with the children. But I like reading very much."

"Were these women—Mrs. Thomas and Mrs. Hammond—kind to you?" asked Marilla.

"They wanted to be kind," Anne said slowly. "But they were always very tired. They couldn't really be kind to me."

Marilla suddenly felt very sorry for Anne. The little girl's life was very sad. Nobody wanted her or loved her.

When Mrs. Spencer saw Marilla and Anne, she was very surprised. Marilla told her about the problem.

"I'm very sorry," answered Mrs. Spencer. "I made a mistake. But I have an idea. My neighbor, Mrs. Blewett, has a new baby. She wants a girl to help her. Anne can go and live with her."

"Oh," said Marilla. She knew about Mrs. Blewett. Mrs. Blewett had a lot of children, but she wasn't very kind to them.

"Look!" said Mrs. Spencer.

"Here's Mrs. Blewett now."

Mrs. Blewett had small, cold eyes.

"This is Marilla Cuthbert from Green Gables," Mrs. Spencer told her. "And this little girl is from the orphanage. I brought her for Marilla but Marilla wants a boy. Would you like her?"

Mrs. Blewett looked at Anne for a long time. She didn't smile. "She's very thin," she said. "I hope she's strong. She'll have to work hard. Yes, Mrs. Spencer, I'll take this girl. She can come home with me now."

Marilla looked at Anne's unhappy face. "I can't give Anne to Mrs. Blewett," she thought. "Wait," she said. "First I have to discuss things with my brother, Matthew. He wants Anne to stay with us."

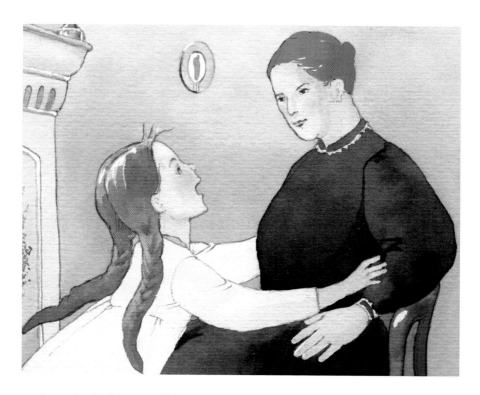

Anne looked at Marilla in surprise. Then she jumped up and ran across the room. "Can I really stay with you at Green Gables?" she asked. "Did you really say that?"

"I don't know," said Marilla. "Now sit down and be quiet."

When Marilla and Anne arrived at Green Gables, Matthew met them. He was very happy when he saw Anne. Later, Marilla told him about Mrs. Blewett. She told him Anne's story, too. Matthew wasn't usually angry, but he was very angry about Mrs. Blewett.

"That Blewett woman is very unkind," he said.

"I know," said Marilla. "I don't like her. All right, Matthew, Anne can stay here with us. But I don't know very much about children. I hope I don't make any mistakes with her."

"Thank you, Marilla," said Matthew happily. "Anne's a very interesting little girl. Be good to her. Then she'll always love you."

CHAPTER 3

Red Hair

"She's very thin, Marilla. And her hair is as red as carrots!
Come here, child. I want to see you."

Next day, Marilla didn't tell Anne about her conversation with Matthew. She gave Anne a lot of work in the kitchen.

"Marilla," said Anne excitedly, "I have to know about my future. Please tell me. Are you going to send me away?"

"No," said Marilla. "You can stay at Green Gables with Matthew and me. But you have to be good."

Anne started to cry.

"Why are you crying?" asked Marilla in surprise. "Don't you want to stay with us? Don't you like Green Gables?"

"Oh, yes, Marilla!" cried Anne. "I like it very much. I'm crying because I'm very happy. And I'll always be good."

Some days later, Mrs. Lynde came to tea with Marilla. When she arrived, Anne was outside. Marilla and Mrs. Lynde sat in the kitchen and talked.

"I think you're making a mistake," said Mrs. Lynde. "You don't know anything about children."

"No, but I can learn," said Marilla.

Anne ran into the kitchen. She saw Mrs. Lynde and stopped.

"The Cuthberts didn't take you for your pretty face!" Mrs. Lynde said. "She's very thin, Marilla. And her hair is as red as **carrot**s! Come here, child. I want to see you."

Anne ran across the kitchen and stood in front of Mrs. Lynde. Her face was red and angry. "I hate you!" she cried. "I hate you—I hate you!"

"Anne!" cried Marilla.

"You're a very **rude** woman," Anne told Mrs. Lynde. "And you're fat!"

carrot /ˈkærət/ (n) A *carrot* is a long, orange vegetable.
rude /rud/ (adj) When you are *rude* to somebody, your words are unkind.

16

"Anne, go to your room!" said Marilla. "Wait for me there!"

Anne started to cry. Then she ran upstairs.

Mrs. Lynde got up from her chair. "I'm going home now, Marilla," she said. "That child is very wild. You'll have a lot of problems with her!"

"But you said unkind things about her!" said Marilla.

After Mrs. Lynde went home, Marilla went upstairs. "Why did Anne say those things?" she thought unhappily. "Now Mrs. Lynde will tell everybody in Avonlea about her."

"Stop crying and listen to me, Anne," she said. "You were very rude to Mrs. Lynde. She was a visitor in my home."

"But she was very unkind," said Anne.

"I want you to say sorry to Mrs. Lynde," said Marilla.

"Never!" said Anne. "I'm not sorry."

Marilla remembered something. When she was a child, her aunts often talked about her. "Marilla isn't a very pretty little girl," they said.

"Maybe Mrs. Lynde was unkind," said Marilla quietly. "But you have to say sorry. Stay here in your room!"

Next morning, Anne didn't come down to breakfast. Marilla told Matthew the story. "She was very rude," she said.

"But, Marilla," said Matthew. "Mrs. Lynde doesn't think before she speaks. Please don't be angry with Anne."

Anne stayed in her room all day. Marilla took food upstairs, but Anne didn't eat very much. In the evening, Matthew went quietly up to Anne's room.

Anne was on a chair by the window. She looked very small and unhappy. Matthew felt very sorry for her. He closed the door. "Please go and say sorry to Mrs. Lynde, Anne," he said.

"All right, Matthew," said Anne. "I wasn't sorry yesterday, but I'm sorry now. I'll do it because you asked me."

"Good," said Matthew happily. "It's very quiet downstairs without you, Anne." He went quietly out of the room.

Later, Marilla and Anne walked to Mrs. Lynde's house.

"I'm very, very sorry, Mrs. Lynde," said Anne. "I was very rude to you. You were right about my red hair. And I *am* thin and ugly."

Mrs. Lynde smiled. "I was rude to you, too," she said. "You *do* have red hair. But maybe it will change color when you're older."

"That's very kind of you, Mrs. Lynde!" said Anne. "Now I can hope for prettier hair. Please can I go outside and play?"

"Yes, of course," said Mrs. Lynde. "Find some flowers."

Anne went out and closed the door behind her.

"Anne is really sorry," thought Marilla. "But she's funny, too."

"She's a strange little girl," said Mrs. Lynde to Marilla. "But she isn't a bad child. I like her."

On the way home, Anne suddenly put her small hand into Marilla's hand. "I love Green Gables, Marilla," she said. "It's my home now."

3.1 Were you right?

Look back at Activity 2.4. Then put these words in the sentences.

be	be	come	die	live	not go	want

Anne's story

Anne [1] ....lived............ in four homes before she [2] ....
to Avonlea. Her parents [3] .... when she was a baby.
After that, nobody [4] .... her or loved her. Nobody
[5] .... kind to her. She [6] .... to school. Her
life [7] .... sad.

3.2 What more did you learn?

1 Number Anne's four homes before Green Gables, 1–4. Start with her first home.

A ☐ Mrs. Hammond's   **C** ☐ the orphanage

B ☐ with her parents   **D** ☐ Mrs. Thomas's

Which will be her next home? Write the number 5.

☐ Mrs. Blewett's   ☐ Mrs. Spencer's

☐ Miss Cuthbert's   ☐ Mrs. Lynde's

2 Who says these things? Who are they talking to?

a "Her hair is as red as carrots!"   .... to ....

b "You're fat!"   .... to ....

c "Marilla isn't a very pretty little girl."   ....

d "Please go and say sorry to Mrs. Lynde."   .... to ....

e "She's a strange little girl. But ... I like her."   .... to ....

3 Do people in your family say rude things about you? What do they say?

....

.3 Language in use

Look at the sentence in the box. It tells us about the day. Then look at this picture of Avonlea.

> The sun shone and the sky was blue.

1 Write these words on the picture.

| horses | birds | fruit | river | sun | chickens | flowers | sky |

2 Now write about the day in the picture.

The sky was blue and the sun shone

....

....

....

....

....

.4 What's next?

In Chapters 4 and 5, Anne goes to church and goes to a party. Then she starts school. The other children laugh at her in church. Why, do you think? Something goes wrong before the party. What? Something goes wrong at school. What? Talk to other students.

CHAPTER 4

The Party

"Anne," Marilla said, "I'll ask you again. "Did you take the brooch from my room and lose it?"

Anne had only one ugly dress from the orphanage. So Marilla made her three new dresses. She bought a little hat for Anne, too. But Anne didn't like the new clothes.

"Why don't you like them, Anne?" asked Marilla.

"They're—they're not—pretty," answered Anne.

"But they're very good dresses," said Marilla.

Marilla went to church every Sunday. She wanted to take Anne with her. But the next Sunday, Marilla was sick.

"Can you go to church without me?" she asked Anne.

"Yes, of course, Marilla," answered Anne.

She put on one of her new dresses and her hat, and started walking down the road to church. "I don't like this hat," she thought. "It isn't very pretty."

Then she had an idea. There were a lot of beautiful yellow flowers by the road. Anne put some flowers on her hat.

When she arrived at church, the other children looked at her. "That girl's crazy!" they said.

After church, Anne ran back to Green Gables.

"Did you enjoy it, Anne?" asked Marilla.

"Not very much," said Anne. "The **minister** talked for a long time, but he wasn't very interesting. But there's going to be a party next week for the children of Avonlea. That's exciting. Please, Marilla, can I go, too?"

"Yes, of course," answered Marilla.

"Oh, thank you, Marilla!" said Anne. She put her arms around Marilla.

Marilla felt happy. "I'm starting to love this child," she thought.

◆

Marilla had a beautiful old **brooch**. The day before the party, she couldn't find it. "It was on top of the desk in my room," she thought. "But now it isn't there. Where is it?"

"Did you take my brooch out of my room?" she asked Anne.

minister /ˈmɪnəstər/ (n) A *minister* works for a church and speaks there on Sundays.
brooch /broʊtʃ, brutʃ/ (n) Women wear *brooches* on their clothes because they want to look pretty.

"No, Marilla," said Anne. "I went into your room last week. I saw the brooch on top of the desk and put it on my dress. But then I put it back on the desk. I didn't take it out of your room."

Marilla looked for the brooch again, but she couldn't find it.

"Anne," she said, "I'll ask you again. Did you take the brooch from my room and lose it?"

"No, I didn't, Marilla," said Anne quietly.

"Go to your room and stay there," said Marilla.

Anne went to her room. Later, Marilla went to see her.

"Marilla, the party is tomorrow," Anne said. "Please can I go?"

"No," said Marilla angrily. "Tell me about the brooch first."

"But I told you about the brooch, Marilla!" cried Anne.

Next morning, Marilla took Anne's breakfast upstairs. Anne sat on her bed. Her face was white and her big gray eyes shone.

"I'll tell you about the brooch now," she said quietly. "I took it and I put it on my dress. Then I went outside and walked down the road to the bridge. I wanted to look at the brooch again, so I took it off my dress. It shone in the sun and was very beautiful. But then it fell from my hand—down, down to the bottom of the river."

"You're a very bad girl, Anne," Marilla said angrily.

"I'm sorry," said Anne. "Please can I go to the party now?"

"The party!" cried Marilla. "Of course you can't go!"

"But, Marilla," said Anne, "you wanted to know about the brooch. So I told you. Now please can I go to the party?"

"No," said Marilla, and went out.

Anne fell on her bed and began to cry.

Marilla went downstairs with a very sad heart. "Maybe Mrs. Lynde was right about Anne," she thought.

After lunch, Marilla wanted to go for a walk. She took her coat from the closet. Then she saw something on her coat. It was her beautiful brooch.

"What's this?" thought Marilla in surprise. "Oh, I remember now. I put the brooch on this coat."

She went to Anne's room. "Anne, why did you tell me that story this morning?" she said. "The brooch is here on my coat."

"I wanted to go to the party," said Anne sadly. "You wanted me to tell you about the brooch. So I had to think of a story."

Marilla began to laugh. "I'm sorry, Anne," she said. "I made a mistake. Now get ready for the party."

"Oh, Marilla!" cried Anne. "Isn't it too late?"

"No," answered Marilla. "It's only two o'clock. Wash your face and put on one of your new dresses. I'll give you some food for the party."

When Anne came home that evening, she was very happy. "Oh, Marilla, the party was wonderful!" she said.

CHAPTER 5

Love and Hate

"I hate you!" Anne cried. She hit Gilbert on the head with her slate and the slate broke.

"Marilla," said Anne one day, "do any other little girls live near Green Gables? I'd like to have a best friend."

"Yes," answered Marilla. "Diana Barry is the same age as you. She lives at Orchard Slope, across the river. I'm going to visit her mother this afternoon. You can come with me."

Mrs. Barry was a tall, thin woman. Diana was a very pretty little girl with black hair and dark eyes. She had a little sister, Minnie May. Minnie May was three years old.

"Diana, take Anne outside," said Mrs. Barry.

Anne and Diana went outside and stood quietly by the flowers. Then they started to talk. They talked all afternoon.

"Did you like Diana, Anne?" asked Marilla later.

"Oh, yes," said Anne happily. "Diana is wonderful!"

Anne and Diana met every day. Sometimes they played in the woods. Sometimes they read books and told stories.

◆

Then summer ended and September came. Anne went to school in Avonlea. She was good at her lessons and she liked the other girls. But Anne didn't like the teacher, Mr. Phillips, very much.

One day, there was a new boy in school. He was tall, with brown hair. The girls liked him.

"That's Gilbert Blythe," Diana said to Anne. "His family went away for the summer. They came back on Saturday."

Gilbert's desk was near Anne's desk. He often looked at her. He wanted her to look at him, too. She was different from the other girls in Avonlea. But Anne wasn't interested in Gilbert.

Gilbert took Anne's hair in his hand. "Carrots!" he said loudly. "Carrots!"

Anne jumped to her feet and looked at Gilbert angrily. "I hate you!" she cried. "I hate you!" She hit Gilbert on the head with her **slate** and the slate broke. Everybody looked at her.

Mr. Phillips ran to her. "Anne Shirley, what are you doing?" he asked. "Answer me!"

"Anne didn't do anything wrong," said Gilbert quickly. "I was rude about her hair."

"Anne, go and stand in front of the class," said Mr. Phillips.

slate /sleɪt/ (n) In past times, children wrote on thin gray *slates* in school. You could wash a *slate* and write on it again.

Anne stood in front of the class all afternoon. Everybody looked at her. But Anne didn't look at anybody. "I'll never speak to Gilbert Blythe again," she thought.

After school Gilbert tried to talk to Anne, but she walked past him.

"Don't be angry with Gilbert, Anne," said Diana. "He laughs at my hair because it's very black."

"Gilbert Blythe was very unkind," said Anne.

The children often played outside after lunch. Sometimes they were late for afternoon school. The next day, Mr. Phillips was in the classroom when Anne arrived with flowers in her hair.

"Anne Shirley, you're late," Mr. Phillips said. "Take those flowers out of your hair. Then go and sit with Gilbert Blythe."

"I can't sit next to Gilbert," Anne thought. "I hate him!"

She got up slowly from her desk and sat down next to Gilbert. But she didn't look at him. She put her head on her arms. A little later, Gilbert pushed some candy under Anne's arm. Anne took the candy and threw it onto the floor.

At the end of the day, Anne took her slate and her books.

"What are you doing, Anne?" asked Diana in surprise.

"I'm taking my things home," said Anne. "I'm going to study there. I'm not coming back to school again."

Later, Anne told Marilla about Mr. Phillips. "I'll learn my lessons at home," she said. "I'll work hard and I'll be a good girl. But I'm not going back to Mr. Phillips."

Marilla went to see Mrs. Lynde. "What shall I do?" she asked.

"Leave Anne at home," said Mrs. Lynde. "She'll get bored. Then she'll *want* to go back to school."

Anne learned her lessons at home. In the evenings she played with Diana. She loved Diana, but she hated Gilbert Blythe.

4.1 Were you right?

Remember your ideas from Activity 3.4. Then circle the best answers.

1 Why do the other children in church think that Anne is crazy?
  a Because her dress isn't pretty.
  b Because she puts wild flowers in her hat.
  c Because she thinks the minister is boring.

2 Before the party, Marilla thinks that Anne lost her brooch. Where is the brooch?
  a At the bottom of the river.
  b On Marilla's desk.
  c On Marilla's coat.

3 When Gilbert laughs at Anne's red hair, what does she do?
  a She cries and runs away.
  b She hits him on the head with a slate.
  c She laughs, too.

4.2 What more did you learn?

1 **What kind of person is Anne? Circle the best words.**

wild
good
bad
rude
crazy
quiet
unkind

different from other children
has strong feelings
the same as other children
gets angry too quickly

2 **Do you remember when you were eleven? In what ways were you the same as / different from Anne? Tell other students.**

Language in use

Look at the sentence in the box. Then finish each sentence below with the best words on the right.

> "The minister talked for a long time, **but** he wasn't very interesting."

1 Marilla looks for the brooch

2 Anne has to tell Marilla about the brooch

3 Anne tells Marilla a story

4 Marilla says sorry to Anne

5 Anne is excited

- so she can go to the party.
- but she can't find it.
- before she can go to the party.
- after she finds the brooch.
- because she can go to the party.

What's next?

Look at the pictures. Circle *will* or *won't* in these sentences.

Diana *will* / *won't* be sick after tea at Green Gables.

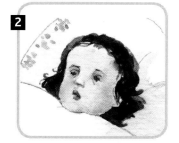

Minnie May *will* / *won't* be sick after Anne's visit.

Anne *will* / *won't* make a cake for Mrs. Allan.

Mrs. Allan *will* / *won't* be sick after her cake.

CHAPTER 6

Diana Comes to Tea

"Anne, what's wrong?" asked Marilla. "Why are you crying?"
"When Diana left here on Saturday, she was drunk!"

"Anne, I'm going out this afternoon," said Marilla one Saturday. "You can invite Diana here for tea. There's cake—and a bottle of fruit **cordial** on a shelf in the kitchen closet."

When Diana arrived, the two little girls played outside.

"I'm very thirsty," said Diana after a time.

"Would you like some fruit cordial?" asked Anne.

She went to the kitchen closet and got the bottle. The cordial was a dark red color. Anne wasn't thirsty, but Diana drank a big glass of it.

cordial /ˈkɔːdʒəl/ (n) *Cordial* is a fruit drink with sugar in it.

"This is very nice," she said. "Can I have another glass?"

After three glasses of cordial, Diana put her hands to her head.

"I'm not feeling very well," she said. "I have to go home."

"But, Diana!" cried Anne sadly. "Don't you want any cake?"

"No," said Diana. "I have to go home now."

The next day, Sunday, it rained all day and Anne stayed at home. On Monday, Marilla sent Anne to Mrs. Lynde's house. But Anne came back very quickly, and ran into the kitchen.

"Anne, what's wrong?" asked Marilla. "Why are you crying?"

"Mrs. Barry was at Mrs. Lynde's house today," said Anne. "She said very bad things about me. When Diana left here on Saturday, she was **drunk**!"

"Drunk!" cried Marilla in surprise. "What did you give her?"

"Only the fruit cordial," answered Anne unhappily. Marilla went to the kitchen closet and found the bottle of cordial. She looked at it. It wasn't fruit cordial. It was red **wine**!

drunk /drʌŋk/ (adj) When you drink a lot of alcohol, you get *drunk*.
wine /waɪn/ (n) *Wine* is a red or white alcoholic drink.

"Oh, no!" she thought. "I remember now. The fruit cordial is in the other closet."

Marilla went to see Mrs. Barry. She tried to tell Mrs. Barry about the mistake, but Mrs. Barry didn't want to listen.

"That Anne Shirley is a very bad little girl," she said. "I don't want Diana to play with her again."

Anne was very sad. She loved Diana very much. Some days later, she went back to school. "I can't be Diana's friend now," Anne told Marilla. "But I can look at her in school."

Anne worked hard. The other girls liked her, and she had a lot of friends. But she was very unhappy about Diana.

One evening some weeks later, Marilla went to a meeting in Charlottetown, the most important town on Prince Edward **Island**. Mrs. Lynde and Diana's parents went to the meeting, too. They all slept in Charlottetown that night.

Anne and Matthew stayed at home. They sat in the kitchen. Anne studied her lessons at the table. Suddenly, Diana ran through the door. Her face was very white.

"Oh, Anne, please come quickly!" she said. "Minnie May is very sick. She has **croup**. Maybe she's going to die."

Matthew got up quietly and put on his coat. "I'll go for the doctor," he said, and went out.

"Don't be afraid, Diana," said Anne. "I know about croup. Mrs. Hammond had eight children and they all had it. Wait! Marilla has some **medicine**. I'll bring it with me."

Anne went with Diana to the Barrys' house. The ground was white with snow. When they arrived at the house, Anne went to Minnie May. She was very sick.

"Now, Diana, bring me hot water," said Anne.

island /ˈaɪlənd/ (n) An *island* is a place with water all around it.
croup /krup/ (n) Children with *croup* were very sick and they often died.
medicine /ˈmɛdəsən/ (n) You take *medicine* when you are sick.

She undressed Minnie May and put her to bed. Then she gave her some medicine. All night Minnie May was very sick, but in the early morning she slept quietly.

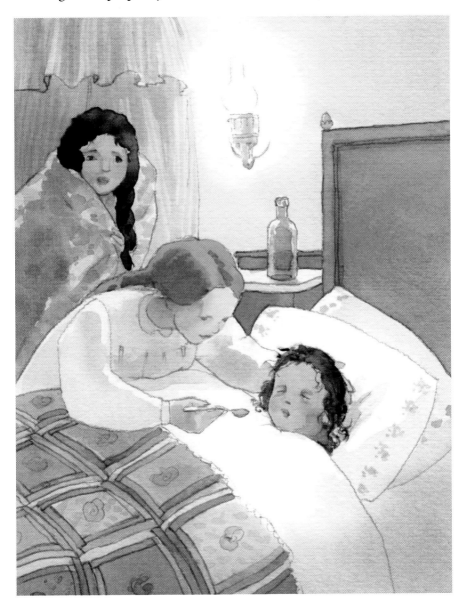

Matthew arrived with the doctor. "I'm sorry we're late," he said. "The doctor wasn't at home. I had to wait for a long time."

The doctor looked at Minnie May. "You did very well, Anne," he said.

Anne drove home with Matthew in the snow. When they arrived at Green Gables, Anne went to bed.

That afternoon, Marilla was downstairs in the kitchen.

"How was the meeting, Marilla?" asked Anne.

"Fine," answered Marilla. "Listen, Anne, Mrs. Barry was here this morning and told me about Minnie May's croup. She wanted to say 'thank you' to you. And she's very sorry about the fruit cordial. She wants you and Diana to be friends again."

"Oh, Marilla, that's wonderful!" cried Anne. "Can I go and see Diana now?"

"Yes," said Marilla, and smiled.

Anne ran quickly to Diana's house. It was cold, and she had no coat or hat. But she was the happiest girl in Avonlea.

CHAPTER 7

A Cake for Mrs. Allan

"Is something wrong?" thought Marilla. She tried some cake, too.
"Anne Shirley!" she cried. "What did you put in this?"

The long summer vacation began at the end of June. Mr. Phillips left the Avonlea school. The old minister left the church, too, and a new minister came. His name was Mr. Allan. He brought his pretty young wife with him.

"I'll ask Mr. and Mrs. Allan to tea on Wednesday," said Marilla.

"Oh, Marilla," said Anne excitedly. "Can I make a cake?"

"All right, Anne," said Marilla.

On Wednesday morning, Anne got up early and made her cake. It looked very good. In the afternoon, Anne put flowers around the table. Then Mr. and Mrs. Allan arrived.

"The table looks beautiful," they said.

Anne felt very happy. She sat at the table with Matthew and Marilla. Matthew wore his best clothes.

"Would you like some cake, Mrs. Allan?" asked Anne. "I made it for you."

"Yes, please," said Mrs. Allan, and she smiled.

Anne cut some cake for Mrs. Allan. Mrs. Allan put the cake in her mouth and started to eat it. But she didn't look very happy.

"Is something wrong?" thought Marilla. She tried some cake, too. "Anne Shirley!" she cried. "What did you put in this?"

"Only—only **vanilla**," answered Anne. She went to the kitchen and brought back a small bottle. On the front of the bottle, it said "Best Vanilla."

vanilla /vəˈnɪlə/ (n) You put *vanilla* in foods like cakes and white ice cream.

Marilla opened the bottle. "This isn't vanilla," she said. "It's medicine. Last week I broke the medicine bottle. I put the medicine into this old vanilla bottle."

"Medicine!" said Anne. "Oh!"

She ran upstairs to her room. She cried and cried.

A little later, Anne heard somebody on the stairs, but she didn't look up. "Oh, Marilla," she said, "I'm very unhappy. Everybody in Avonlea will hear about my cake. They'll laugh at me. I can't go downstairs. I can't look at Mrs. Allan again. I'm very sorry, Marilla. Please tell Mrs. Allan."

"You tell her, Anne," said Mrs. Allan.

Anne looked up. "Mrs. Allan!" she said in surprise.

"Yes, it's me," said Mrs. Allan, and laughed. "Don't cry, Anne. The medicine in the cake was a very funny mistake."

"I'm sorry, Mrs. Allan," said Anne. "I wanted to make a nice cake for you."

"I know," said Mrs. Allan. "Now please come down and show me your flowers. I'm very interested in flowers."

Anne felt happy again. She went downstairs with Mrs. Allan and nobody said anything about the cake.

A week later, Anne ran into the kitchen at Green Gables. She was very excited. She had a letter in her hand.

"Mrs. Allan is inviting me to tea tomorrow afternoon," she said. "Look at this letter, Marilla. It says, 'Miss Anne Shirley, Green Gables.' Nobody called me 'Miss' before."

The next afternoon, Anne went to tea with Mrs. Allan.

"I had a wonderful time with Mrs. Allan," she told Marilla later. "She's very kind. And she wore a beautiful dress. We talked for a long time. I told her about Mrs. Thomas and Mrs. Hammond, and the orphanage. I told her about Green Gables and the school, too.

"Mrs. Allan told me something interesting. A new teacher is coming to Avonlea after the vacation. Her name is Miss Muriel Stacy. Isn't that a pretty name? I want to meet her very much."

5.1 Were you right?

1 Look back at Activity 4.4. Then answer this question. Which of these were important in Chapters 6 and 7?

2 Put the right words in these sentences.

a Anne gives Diana three glasses of ....

b Anne thinks it is ....

c After Anne gives Minnie some of Marilla's .... , Minnie feels better.

d Anne puts .... in the cake.

e Marilla put .... in the .... bottle.

3 Who makes the mistakes in Chapters 6 and 7—Anne or Marilla?

....

5.2 What more did you learn?

Which comes first? Number these sentences, 1–7.

a Anne and Diana run to the Barrys' house.

b Anne gets Marilla's medicine from the closet.

c Diana suddenly runs into the kitchen at Green Gables.

1 **d** Marilla, Mrs. Lynde, and Diana's parents go to Charlottetown for a meeting.

e She tells Anne and Matthew that Minnie is very sick.

f When the doctor comes, Minnie is better.

g With hot water and medicine, Anne helps Minnie.

3 Language in use

1 Look at the sentence in the box. Then put these words in the sentences below.

> "I **have to** go home now."

| have to | can | can't | will |

a Anne knows that she .... be Diana's friend now.

b Diana .... run to Matthew and Anne for help with Minnie.

c Matthew says that he .... go for the doctor.

d Matthew .... wait a long time for the doctor.

e Anne .... use hot water and medicine before she makes Minnie better.

f Now Anne .... be friends with Diana again.

2 Work with another student and have this conversation.

Student A: You are Mrs. Lynde. Tell your neighbor about Anne and Minnie and Anne and Mrs. Allan.

Student B: You are Mrs. Lynde's neighbor. Ask questions. Use *could* and *did ... have to* in your questions.

.4 What's next?

Chapter 8 is "An Accident and a New Dress." What do you think?

Who will have an accident? ....

Who will have a new dress? ....

Who will buy it? ....

An Accident and a New Dress

"Who can climb up to the top of Diana's house?"
"I can!" cried Anne. She ran to the house.

S ome weeks later, Diana had a party. She invited Anne and the other girls in her class. They had a very good time.

After tea, the girls played outside. "Let's play a new game," said one of the girls. "Let's do exciting things. Who can climb the big tree by Diana's front door?"

One of the girls climbed the tree. Then another girl thought of something more exciting. "Who can climb up to the top of Diana's house?" she said.

"I can!" cried Anne. She ran to the house.

"Stop, Anne!" called Diana. "That's very dangerous!"

Anne started to climb to the top of the house, but it was very difficult. Suddenly, she fell to the ground.

Diana ran to her. "Oh, Anne, Anne, are you dead?" she said.

Anne opened her eyes. Her face was very white. "No, I'm not dead, Diana," she said. "But my leg hurts. I can't walk."

Mr. Barry carried Anne home to Green Gables. When Marilla saw Mr. Barry with Anne in his arms, she felt very afraid. Was Anne dead?

"I love Anne very much," she thought. "I know that now." She ran to Mr. Barry. "What happened?" she asked.

"Don't be afraid, Marilla," said Anne. "I fell off Diana's house."

Anne couldn't go back to school. She stayed home for seven weeks. Her friends came to see her every day. They brought her flowers and books. She had many other visitors, too. Mrs. Allan and Mrs. Lynde came often.

◆

When Anne's leg was better, she went back to school. She liked Miss Stacy very much. Miss Stacy was a very good young teacher, and Anne worked hard in her lessons.

"I love Miss Stacy," Anne said to Marilla and Matthew one evening. "She wants us to give a **concert** at Christmas. Isn't that exciting? Diana's going to sing a song. And I'm going to say two **poem**s."

One evening, Matthew went into the kitchen at Green Gables. Anne's friends were there. They laughed and talked about the concert. They were very excited.

Matthew watched them. "Anne looks different from the other girls. But why?" he thought. He thought all evening, then suddenly he knew the answer. "Anne's clothes are different," he thought. "The other girls wear pretty dresses. Marilla makes good dresses for Anne, but they aren't very pretty."

Then Matthew had an idea. "I'm going to give Anne a new dress for Christmas," he thought.

He went to the store in town and tried to buy a dress. But he couldn't because he didn't know much about girls' dresses.

---

concert /ˈkɒnsət/ (n) When you go to a *concert*, you hear music.
poem /ˈpoʊəm/ (n) When you write a *poem*, you usually write short lines and beautiful words.

"Maybe somebody can *make* a pretty dress for Anne," he thought. "But who? I don't know many women in Avonlea. I can't ask Marilla. I know—I'll have to ask Mrs. Lynde."

He went to see Mrs. Lynde.

"Of course I'll help you, Matthew," said Mrs. Lynde. "And I won't tell Marilla. It'll be a surprise."

On Christmas morning, Anne woke up early. She looked out of the window and felt very happy. The trees were white with snow.

She ran downstairs into the kitchen and Matthew gave her the dress. Anne started to cry.

"What's wrong?" said Matthew. "Don't you like it?"

"Oh yes, Matthew," answered Anne. "I love the dress. It's beautiful. Thank you! I'm crying because I'm very happy."

That night, Anne wore her new dress to the concert. She said her two poems very well. Matthew and Marilla were at the concert, too. Later, they sat by the kitchen fire and talked.

"Anne did very well tonight," said Matthew.

"Yes," said Marilla. "She's very smart. And she looked very nice in her new dress."

"She's thirteen now," said Matthew. "One day she'll leave the Avonlea school. We have to think about her future."

CHAPTER 9

Some Stupid Mistakes

Marilla looked at Anne's hair. It was green!
"Anne Shirley!" she said. "What did you do to it?"

One spring afternoon, Marilla walked home. The country was very beautiful and Marilla felt happy.

"Anne's at home," she thought. "She'll make a good fire, and she'll have tea on the table."

But Anne wasn't at Green Gables. There was no fire, and the tea wasn't ready.

"Where *is* that girl?" thought Marilla angrily. "Is she playing with Diana again? She has to do housework first."

Matthew came in from the farm and he and Marilla had tea. But Anne didn't come. When it was dark, Marilla went upstairs to Anne's room. Anne was on her bed.

"What's wrong, Anne?" said Marilla in surprise. "Are you sick?"

"No, Marilla," said Anne unhappily. "Look at my hair!"

Marilla looked at Anne's hair. It was green! "Anne Shirley!" she said. "What did you do to it?"

"I **dye**d it," said Anne. "I hated my red hair. Today a man came to Green Gables. He wanted to sell us things. I saw a bottle of black hair dye in his box, so I bought it. But it made my hair green!"

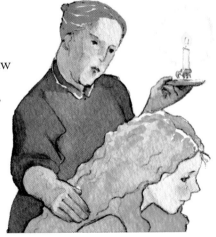

"Go and wash it," said Marilla.

Anne washed her hair. But the green color didn't go away.

"Oh, Marilla," she said. "What shall I do? The other girls will laugh at me. I can't go to school."

dye /daɪ/ (v/n) You *dye* clothes or your hair when you want to change the color.

Anne stayed home for a week.
She washed her hair every day, but
the green color stayed in her hair.

"We'll have to cut it," Marilla said, and
she cut Anne's hair short.

"I'll never hate my red hair again!" Anne said.

She went back to school. When her friends saw her
short hair, they were very surprised. But Anne didn't tell
them about the dye. After some weeks, Anne's hair looked
prettier than before, and it wasn't as red.

◆

One day in the summer, Anne and her friends were by the river
near Diana's house. There was an old boat there.

"Let's play a game," said Anne. "Do you remember that poem
from school about a girl, Elaine? She was unhappy in love. She
found a boat on the river and got into it. Then she died. The river
carried the boat to a town. Everybody came and saw her.

"I'll be Elaine. I'll get into this old boat and the river will carry it
down to the bridge. Go and wait for me there."

Anne climbed into the bottom of the boat. The girls put flowers into
her hands and Anne closed her eyes.

"Oh," said the girls. "Anne really looks dead."

They pushed the boat out into the center of the river, and ran to the
bridge. The river was very fast and dangerous. The boat was old and not
very strong. Suddenly, a lot of water came into the boat. Anne sat up. She
was very afraid.

The boat went past a large tree and Anne caught the tree with her
hands. The river carried the boat away. Then the boat went down—down
to the bottom of the river.

Diana and the other girls waited at the bridge. They saw the boat in
the river, but they didn't see Anne. "Anne's in the river!" they cried. "Let's
go for help!" They ran quickly to Diana's house.

Anne was very cold and wet. She had her arms around the tree, but she couldn't move. Her arms hurt and she felt very tired. "Help! Help!" she cried. "Why doesn't somebody come?"

Suddenly, a small boat came down the river. A boy was in it. It was Gilbert Blythe.

"Anne Shirley, what are you doing here?" he asked in surprise.

Anne told him, and Gilbert brought his boat near the tree. He gave Anne his hand and pulled her into his boat. But Anne didn't look at him.

"Thank you," she said coldly.

"Please, let's be friends," said Gilbert. "I was rude about your hair in school, and I'm sorry. But your hair is very pretty now."

"No," said Anne. "I'll never be friends with you!"

"All right," said Gilbert angrily. "I'll never ask you again!"

6.1 Were you right?

Look back at Activity 5.4. Then circle the best words in *italics*.

1 The girls at Diana's party want to do something more *exciting / dangerous*.

2 Matthew wants Anne to look *different from / the same as* the other girls.

3 Anne cries on Christmas morning because she *hates / loves* the dress.

4 The boat is too *old / strong* and the river is too *fast / wide*.

5 Anne has her arms around *a tree / the boat* when Gilbert comes down the river.

6 Anne and Gilbert *can / can't* be friends now.

6.2 What more did you learn?

What can you see? Write a sentence under each picture. What comes first? Number the pictures, 1–4.

3 Language in use

1 Look at the sentences in the box. Then put 's or s' in the right places below.

> Matthew didn't know much about girls' dresses.
>
> Anne's leg was better.

a Matthew knew about boys clothes.

b Annes visitors bring her flowers and books.

c Annes clothes are different from her friends clothes.

d The mans hair dye makes Annes hair green.

2 Look at the sentences in the box. Then put the right word, with -er or more, in the sentences below.

> Anne's hair looked **prettier** than before.
>
> Another girl thought of something **more exciting**.

beautiful	fast
short	friendly

a The dresses of the other girls were .... than Anne's.

b Anne's hair is .... than her friends' hair.

c The river is .... than the girls think.

d Gilbert is .... than Anne.

4 What's next?

Why doesn't Anne want to be friends with Gilbert? Do you think she will talk to him before the end of the story? Talk to other students. Write your ideas here.

Notes

CHAPTER 10

The Queen's College Class

When Marilla looked at Anne, she felt a little sad.
"She's fifteen now," she thought. "She's almost a woman!"

It was November. Marilla and Anne sat in the kitchen at Green Gables.
Marilla's eyes were tired and weak. They often hurt her.

"I'll go to town tomorrow and get new glasses," she thought.

Anne was in front of the fire with a book in her hand. Marilla
watched her. She loved Anne very much. She often made pretty dresses
for the child now.

"Anne," she said. "Miss Stacy was here today. She talked to me about your future. Would you like to study at Queen's College in Charlottetown? Would you like to be a teacher?"

"Oh yes, Marilla," said Anne, and her eyes shone. "But isn't Queen's College very expensive?"

"Yes," said Marilla. "But Matthew and I will pay for you."

Six other students from Avonlea wanted to go to Queen's College, too. They studied after school in one class—the Queen's College class.

Anne and Gilbert Blythe were the smartest students in the class. Sometimes Anne was first, and sometimes Gilbert. Gilbert was friendly with the other girls in the class, but he never spoke to Anne.

When Anne thought about him, she felt sorry. "I don't hate Gilbert now," she thought.

The Queen's College class was very interesting and the days went quickly. Winter came again, then spring, then summer. At the beginning of the long summer vacation, Anne went home and put her books away in a box.

"I'm not going to study in the vacation," she said to Marilla. "I want to enjoy this summer. There are going to be parties and concerts. And Mr. Barry is going to take us to dinner one evening at the hotel at White Sands."

Mrs. Lynde came to tea with Marilla at Green Gables. "Matthew doesn't look very well these days," she said.

"No," said Marilla. "He had a problem with his heart last week. He works hard, but he has to be careful."

"When Anne came to Green Gables, I said unkind things about her," said Mrs. Lynde. "But I made a big mistake. She helps you, and she's very pretty now, too."

Anne enjoyed her summer very much. In the fall, she went back to school. The Queen's College class started again and Anne worked hard all year. But she went to parties and concerts, too.

When Marilla looked at Anne, she felt a little sad. "She's fifteen now," she thought. "She's almost a woman!"

◆

By June, Anne and the other students were ready for the Queen's College **examination**s. They went to Charlottetown and stayed there for a week. When Anne came home, Diana was at Green Gables.

"How were the examinations, Anne?" she asked.

"They were very difficult," said Anne. "I'm very tired now!"

One evening three weeks later, Anne sat by the window in Green Gables. The summer evening was very beautiful. The sky in the west was slowly turning red.

Suddenly, Diana arrived with a newspaper in her hand. "Anne!" she cried excitedly. "Your name's in the newspaper! You came first in the Queen's College examinations—you and Gilbert Blythe. You're the best students on the island!"

Anne looked at the newspaper. There were two hundred names there. Her name was at the top—hers and Gilbert's!

"This is wonderful, Diana!" she said happily.

She ran to Marilla and Matthew. Then she went to see Mrs. Lynde and Mrs. Allan. "You did very well, Anne," they said.

examination /ɪɡˌzæmə'neɪʃən/ (n) An *examination* is an important test.

CHAPTER 11

A New Start

"Gilbert knows you want to be near Marilla.
The Avonlea school is yours."

Anne went to Queen's College and enjoyed her time there. She was in the same class as Gilbert Blythe, but they didn't speak.

At the end of the year, there were more examinations. Anne did very well. She won a free place at another college, Redmond College. Gilbert Blythe got a place at the college, too.

Anne went back to Green Gables in June. Diana came to see her.

"I have three months' wonderful vacation at Green Gables," said Anne. "Then I'm going to Redmond College."

"Gilbert Blythe isn't going," Diana told her. "His father doesn't have the money. So Gilbert is going to teach in the Avonlea school."

"Oh," said Anne. Suddenly, she felt sad.

The next morning at breakfast, Anne watched Matthew's face. It was very tired and gray.

"Is Matthew all right?" she asked Marilla later.

"No," said Marilla. "He's having problems with his heart again. He works hard, and his heart isn't strong."

Some days later, Matthew came into the kitchen and fell to the ground. Anne and Marilla ran to him. But Matthew was dead.

Anne was very sad. Later, in her room, she cried and cried.

"Matthew was my first friend," she thought. "He brought me to Green Gables. He was always very kind to me. I loved him."

Anne woke in the night and Marilla came to her. "Don't cry," she said. "Matthew was a good brother and a wonderful man. But you have me and I have you, Anne. I love you very much."

◆

Marilla sat at the kitchen table. She looked very tired and sad.

Anne put her arms around her. "What's wrong, Marilla?" she asked.

"My eyes are hurting again," answered Marilla. "I can't see very well and I can't work. And, Anne, there's something worse. I have to sell Green Gables. Matthew and I had our money in the Abbey Bank. But the bank had problems and now there's no money." She started to cry.

"Don't cry, Marilla!" cried Anne. "You don't have to sell Green Gables. You and Matthew did everything for me. Now I'm going to help you. I'm not going to go to Redmond College. I'll teach at a school on Prince Edward Island, and I'll help you with Green Gables. We'll be very happy—you and I."

Mrs. Lynde visited Green Gables. "You're doing a very good thing for Marilla," she said to Anne. "She's very happy. And you can teach at the Avonlea school."

"I can't," said Anne. "Gilbert Blythe is going to teach here. I'll live at Green Gables, but I have to find another school."

"No," said Mrs. Lynde. "Gilbert heard about Marilla's problems. He knows you want to be near Marilla. So he's going to go to the White Sands school. The Avonlea school is yours."

"That's very nice of Gilbert," thought Anne in surprise.

Two days later, Anne met Gilbert on the road. She stopped and put out her hand. "Gilbert," she said, "thank you very much for the job at the Avonlea school. I'm sorry about everything. Please, let's be friends now."

"Yes," said Gilbert, and took Anne's hand. "I'd like that."

Gilbert walked home with Anne. They stood outside Green Gables and talked for half an hour.

Later, Anne sat by her window and looked out. It was a beautiful night. "I know I'm going to be very happy," she thought. "I have a good job and dear friends. Everything is going to be all right."

1 **Work with another student. Look at the pictures and then have this conversation.**

| Student A: | You are Marilla. You and Mathew are sitting in the kitchen when Anne is away. You are talking about her time with you. When was she bad? When was she stupid? |

| Student B: | You are Matthew. Talk about Anne's time with you. When was she good? When was she kind? |

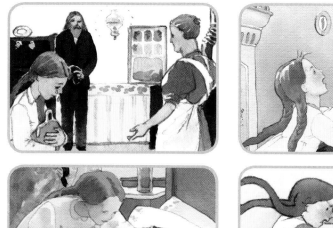

2 **Work with three other students. What did you do when you were younger? Tell a funny story. Which is the best of the four stories? Tell it to the class.**

Anne of Green Gables **follows Anne from the age of eleven to sixteen. At the end of the story she starts a new life. Think about these questions, and then write the next chapter in her story.**

- Where will Anne live?
- Where will she work?
- Who will work on the farm?
- Will Marilla have any money?

- Will Anne make any mistakes?
- Will she see Gilbert or Diana?
- Will she meet new people?

....

....

....

....

....

....

....

....

....

....

....

....

....

....

....

....

....

....

....

....

1 You and two other students work for PEI Vacations in Charlottetown, Nova Scotia. Two families want to come to the island for a vacation. Read their letter and make notes below.

Dear Sir/Madam

We are coming to Prince Edward Island for four days and would like your help with our vacation.
We are two British families (four parents and four children, from twelve to forty years old).
The children love water sports and animals; the parents like water sports and walking.

We all love Anne of Green Gables. We do not have much money. We will arrive at Charlottetown Airport in the early morning of June 6 after we change airplanes in Halifax.
Yours

E. B. Jones

PEI Vacations
Customer Information

Prince Edward Island

Number of people: .... Country ....

Ages: .... Vacation dates: ....

Arriving at: .... by: ....

What do they want to do and see?

....

....

....

Prince Edward Island

Cavendish *Cavendish Beach*

French River   Green Gables House

airport

N
W   E
S

Avonlea
..... End to End Walk

Charlottetown

Read about Prince Edward Island and find the places on the map. Then talk about the best places for the British visitors.

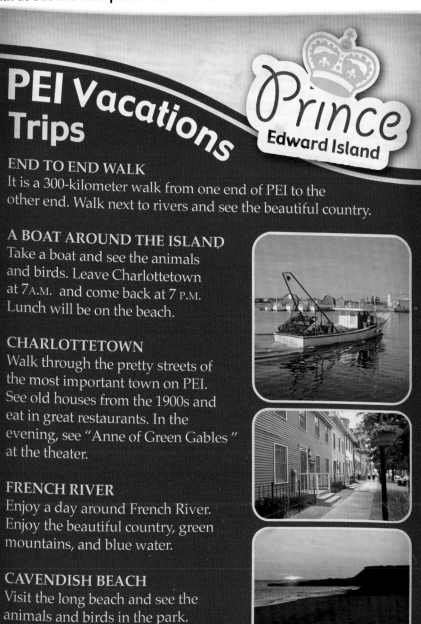

PEI Vacations Trips

Prince Edward Island

END TO END WALK
It is a 300-kilometer walk from one end of PEI to the other end. Walk next to rivers and see the beautiful country.

A BOAT AROUND THE ISLAND
Take a boat and see the animals and birds. Leave Charlottetown at 7 A.M. and come back at 7 P.M. Lunch will be on the beach.

CHARLOTTETOWN
Walk through the pretty streets of the most important town on PEI. See old houses from the 1900s and eat in great restaurants. In the evening, see "Anne of Green Gables" at the theater.

FRENCH RIVER
Enjoy a day around French River. Enjoy the beautiful country, green mountains, and blue water.

CAVENDISH BEACH
Visit the long beach and see the animals and birds in the park. Swim and fish.

3 Which two "Anne of Green Gables" places would the families like to visit?

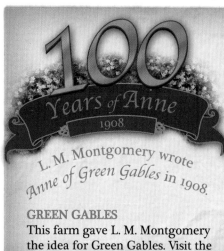

100 Years of Anne 1908

L. M. Montgomery wrote *Anne of Green Gables* in 1908.

GREEN GABLES
This farm gave L. M. Montgomery the idea for Green Gables. Visit the house, store, and restaurant.

AVONLEA
Meet Anne, Gilbert, Marilla, Matthew, and the other people from Green Gables in 1800s Avonlea. Sit in a lesson at Avonlea School. Take a drive in Matthew's horse and buggy. Eat cake and drink fruit cordial. Listen to island music.

HOUSE OF L. M. MONTGOMERY
The famous writer lived in Cavendish from 1876 to 1911 with her grandmother and grandfather. She was an orphan, too. Visit the book store and buy more books about Anne.

4 Plan the vacation for the visitors.

PEI Vacations Plan

Prince Edward Island

DAY 1: .. Arrive Charlottetown Airport and go to hotel ....

....

DAY 2: ....

....

DAY 3: ....

....

DAY 4: ....

....